# Shifting the Scale: Insights on Gender Favoritism

**BY**

**AUGUSTINE  OLISEL**

# Table of Contents

# Introduction

## The Importance of Understanding Gender Dynamics

In our rapidly evolving world, the discussion around gender dynamics has never been more crucial. Understanding how societal norms, historical contexts, and cultural influences shape our perceptions of gender is essential for fostering a more equitable society. The disparities in treatment and expectations for men and women have profound implications on individual lives and collective progress. By delving into the roots and repercussions of these gender dynamics, we can begin to dismantle biases and promote a culture of true equality.

Gender favoritism, whether toward men or women, creates an imbalance that affects every aspect of society—from personal relationships to professional opportunities. It's imperative to recognize and address these imbalances to ensure that all individuals, regardless of gender, can thrive. By understanding the underlying causes and manifestations of gender favoritism, we can work towards a society that values and respects all its members equally.

# Objective of the Book

"Shifting the Scale: Insights on Gender Favoritism" aims to explore the multifaceted nature of gender favoritism and provide a comprehensive analysis that both educates and inspires. This book is not about placing blame or asserting the superiority of one gender over another. Instead, it seeks to offer a balanced perspective that highlights the importance of mutual respect and understanding.

Our objective is to:

1. **Educate**: Provide a thorough understanding of the historical and cultural contexts that have shaped current gender dynamics.

2. **Inspire**: Draw on the insights of philosophers and preachers of love to offer inspirational messages and guidance for achieving gender balance.

3. **Encourage Reflection**: Prompt readers to reflect on their own perceptions and biases, fostering a more conscious approach to gender equality.

4. **Promote Change**: Suggest practical strategies and reforms that can help in addressing and mitigating gender biases in various aspects of society.

# Overview of Themes

The themes explored in this book are diverse yet interconnected, each shedding light on different aspects of gender favoritism:

1. **Historical Context**: Analyzing how gender roles have evolved over time and the lasting impact of historical gender norms.

2. **Modern Society**: Examining contemporary gender perceptions and the influence of societal structures on gender favoritism.

3. **Education and Workforce**: Exploring gender dynamics in education and professional environments, highlighting both challenges and progress.

4. **Media and Culture**: Investigating the role of media and cultural narratives in shaping and perpetuating gender stereotypes.

5. **Emotional Well-being**: Addressing the emotional and mental health implications of gender expectations.

6. **Legal Frameworks**: Evaluating the impact of laws and policies on gender equality.

7. **Relationships**: Understanding gender dynamics within personal relationships and the quest for equality.

8. **Religion and Spirituality**: Analyzing religious teachings and spiritual insights on gender equality.

9. **Path Forward**: Proposing actionable strategies for achieving gender balance and fostering a more equitable society.

Each chapter is designed to be thoughtful, educational, and inspirational, offering a blend of theoretical insights and practical advice. By incorporating the wisdom of philosophers and the compassionate teachings of preachers of love, this book aspires to be a beacon of hope and a guide for those committed to gender equality.

# Chapter One

# Historical Context of Gender Roles

## Ancient Societies and Gender Roles

The roles and expectations of genders have been deeply embedded in human societies since the dawn of civilization. In ancient societies, these roles were largely shaped by practical considerations related to survival and efficiency. Men, generally physically stronger, were often hunters, warriors, and protectors, while women, who bore and nurtured children, tended to focus on domestic responsibilities and gathering resources. These roles were not merely about physical capabilities but were also influenced by the spiritual and cultural beliefs of the time.

In ancient Egypt, for example, women had a relatively high status and enjoyed legal rights similar to men. They could own property, initiate divorce, and were even seen in positions of power, such as Pharaoh Hatshepsut and Cleopatra. This relative gender equity was unique compared to other ancient civilizations.

In contrast, ancient Greece exhibited a more patriarchal structure. While women were essential in religious rituals and domestic spheres, their roles were highly restricted in public and political life. The philosopher Aristotle famously argued that women were naturally inferior to men, an idea that heavily influenced Western thought for centuries.

Ancient India presented a complex tapestry of gender roles, often defined by religious and social structures. The Manusmriti, an ancient legal text, outlined specific duties and behaviors for men and women, often placing women in a subordinate position. However, periods like the Vedic Age saw women participating in scholarly and spiritual activities, indicating that gender roles were not always rigid.

## Evolution of Gender Norms Through Ages

As societies evolved, so did their perceptions and norms regarding gender. The Middle Ages, influenced by feudal systems and the dominance of the Church, reinforced patriarchal norms. Women's roles were largely confined to the home, and their primary identity was often linked to their relationships with men—either as daughters, wives, or mothers.

During the Renaissance, there was a slight shift as some women, primarily in noble families, gained access to education and participated in intellectual pursuits. Figures like Isabella d'Este and Artemisia Gentileschi broke through societal constraints, yet the broader societal roles for women remained largely restrictive.

The Industrial Revolution marked a significant turning point. As economies shifted from agrarian to industrial, women began to enter the workforce in greater numbers, particularly in textile factories. This economic necessity challenged traditional gender roles, although it also led to the exploitation of women and children in harsh working conditions.

The 20th century witnessed dramatic changes with the advent of women's suffrage movements and feminist ideologies. Women in many parts of the world fought for and gained the right to vote, access to education, and equal employment opportunities. The world wars further accelerated this shift as women took on roles traditionally held by men, proving their capability in various fields.

Philosophers throughout history have both reinforced and challenged prevailing gender norms. Their writings provide valuable insights into the evolving perceptions of gender roles.

1. **Plato**: Unlike his student Aristotle, Plato in his work "The Republic" proposed a radical idea for his time—that women, given the same education and opportunities, could perform roles in society just as effectively as men. He advocated for the inclusion of women in his ideal society's guardian class, emphasizing their potential for reason and leadership.

2. **Confucius**: In contrast, Confucian philosophy, which deeply influenced East Asian cultures, emphasized a clear hierarchy and distinct roles for men and women. The Confucian ideal of the "three obediences and four virtues" dictated that a woman should obey her father, husband, and son, and excel in virtue, speech, appearance, and work.

3. **Mary Wollstonecraft**: An early advocate for women's rights, Wollstonecraft's seminal work "A Vindication of the Rights of Woman" (1792)

argued for the education of women and their right to participate equally in society. She challenged the prevailing notion that women were inherently inferior and asserted that their perceived inferiority was a result of lack of education and opportunity.

4. **John Stuart Mill**: In "The Subjection of Women" (1869), Mill argued passionately for gender equality, criticizing the legal and social restrictions placed on women. He viewed the subjugation of women as a hindrance to human progress and advocated for their equal participation in all aspects of society.

5. **Simone de Beauvoir**: In her groundbreaking work "The Second Sex" (1949), Beauvoir explored the construction of women's roles and identities through a patriarchal lens. She famously stated, "One is not born, but rather becomes, a woman," highlighting the social and cultural factors that shape gender roles.

## Intersection of Gender and Power Structures

Gender roles have always been intertwined with power structures, whether political, economic, or religious. In many societies, patriarchal systems have used gender roles to maintain control and reinforce hierarchies.

In feudal Europe, the control of land and resources was tightly linked to gender. Men, as heads of households and lords, held power over property and people, while women's roles were largely supportive. Marriage alliances were strategic, consolidating wealth and influence within patriarchal frameworks.

Religious institutions also played a critical role. For instance, the Catholic Church, with its all-male priesthood and emphasis on female modesty and subservience, reinforced gender hierarchies. However, women found spaces within these constraints to exert influence, such as through religious orders or as mystics and saints.

Colonialism further complicated gender dynamics, as European powers imposed their own gender norms on colonized societies. Indigenous gender roles, which were often more fluid and equitable, were suppressed in favor of European patriarchal structures. This imposition disrupted traditional practices and contributed to long-lasting inequalities.

# Gender Roles in Non-Western Societies

Exploring non-Western societies reveals diverse approaches to gender roles. Many indigenous cultures, for example, had more fluid and egalitarian gender norms. In Native American tribes, Two-Spirit people, who embodied both masculine and feminine qualities, held respected positions in their communities. These roles were not strictly binary and reflected a broader understanding of gender.

In many African societies, gender roles were also complex and varied widely. Women often held significant economic power, particularly in agricultural and trading activities. The matrilineal societies of West Africa, where lineage and inheritance were traced through the mother, offered a different perspective on gender roles compared to patriarchal systems.

Asian societies, influenced by Confucianism, Buddhism, and other philosophies, had their own distinct gender norms. In Japan, the concept of "Onna Daigaku" (Great Learning for Women) emphasized traditional roles of wifehood and motherhood, yet women in samurai families managed households and even engaged in martial training. The presence of powerful female figures like Empress Wu Zetian in China or Queen Seondeok in Korea also showcased the nuanced roles women could play.

## Conclusion: Lessons from History

The historical context of gender roles teaches us that these norms are neither static nor universal. They have been shaped by practical needs, cultural beliefs, religious doctrines, and power dynamics. Understanding this evolution is crucial for addressing contemporary gender biases.

While progress has been made, the remnants of historical gender norms still influence modern societies. By examining the past, we can better understand the origins of current disparities and work towards a more equitable future. Philosophers and historical figures have provided valuable insights, challenging us to question and redefine gender roles. As we move forward, drawing lessons from history can guide us in creating a society that truly values and respects all individuals, regardless of gender.

# Chapter Two

## Modern Society and Gender Perceptions

<u>Contemporary Gender Roles</u>

In modern society, gender roles have undergone significant transformation, yet the legacy of historical norms continues to influence contemporary perceptions. Today, there is a greater emphasis on gender equality and fluidity, challenging the traditional binary understanding of gender. However, these shifts vary widely across different cultures and regions, reflecting a complex interplay of progress and resistance.

In many Western societies, the feminist movements of the 20th and 21st centuries have been instrumental in advocating for women's rights and gender equality. These movements have brought about crucial changes in legal frameworks, workplace policies, and cultural attitudes. The push for equal pay, reproductive rights, and against gender-based violence are just a few areas where significant progress has been made. Yet, despite these advancements, issues such as the gender pay gap, underrepresentation in leadership positions, and pervasive stereotypes remain.

In contrast, some cultures and regions still adhere to more traditional gender roles, often influenced by religious and cultural beliefs. For example, in parts of the Middle East and South Asia, patriarchal norms are deeply entrenched, and women may face significant barriers in accessing education, employment, and political participation. Efforts to address these issues are ongoing, with grassroots organizations and international bodies advocating for gender equality.

In addition, the recognition and acceptance of non-binary and transgender identities have added new dimensions to the discussion on gender roles. Activists and scholars emphasize that gender is not merely a binary construct but a spectrum. This understanding challenges deeply rooted societal norms and calls for inclusive policies and practices that respect individual identities.

<u>**Societal Structures and Gender Favoritism**</u>

Societal structures play a crucial role in perpetuating or challenging gender favoritism. These structures include family dynamics, educational systems, workplace environments, and media representation.

**Family Dynamics:** Traditional family structures often reinforce specific gender roles, with expectations for men and women being markedly different. In many cultures, men are still viewed as the primary breadwinners, while women are often expected to take on the bulk of caregiving and household responsibilities. This division of labor can limit opportunities for women to pursue careers and for men to engage fully in family life.

However, there is a growing trend towards more egalitarian family models. In many households, both parents share economic and caregiving responsibilities. Policies such as paternity leave and flexible working hours support this shift, allowing men to participate more actively in family life and women to advance in their careers.

**Educational Systems:** Education is a powerful tool for challenging gender norms and promoting equality. In many parts of the world, there has been significant progress in closing the gender gap in education. Girls are enrolling in schools and universities at higher rates, and there is a growing emphasis on STEM (Science, Technology, Engineering, and Mathematics) education for girls.

Despite these advancements, gender biases persist in educational content and practices. Textbooks may still portray stereotypical gender roles, and teachers' expectations can influence students' subject choices and performance. Encouraging critical thinking and inclusivity in education can help dismantle these biases.

**Workplace Environments:** The workplace is another critical arena where gender favoritism can manifest. Issues such as the gender pay gap, lack of representation in leadership positions, and discrimination remain prevalent. Women, particularly those of color or from marginalized communities, often face multiple layers of bias and barriers.

Many organizations are implementing policies to address these issues, including diversity and inclusion training, mentorship programs, and transparent pay structures. However, creating a truly equitable workplace requires a cultural shift that values diversity and challenges entrenched norms.

**Media Representation:** Media plays a significant role in shaping societal perceptions of gender. From advertisements to movies to news coverage, the representation of men and women can reinforce or challenge stereotypes. Historically, media has often portrayed women in limited roles, emphasizing beauty and domesticity, while men are depicted as strong, decisive, and dominant.

There is a growing movement towards more nuanced and diverse representations of gender in the media. Campaigns like MeToo and TimesUp have highlighted issues of harassment and inequality, pushing for greater accountability and representation. Media literacy programs also encourage critical engagement with media content, helping individuals recognize and challenge biased portrayals.

Philosophers and contemporary thinkers continue to provide valuable insights into the complexities of modern gender issues. Their work challenges us to reflect on our assumptions and consider new perspectives.

**Judith Butler:** Butler's concept of gender performativity, introduced in "Gender Trouble" (1990), argues that gender is not an innate quality but a performance shaped by societal norms. This perspective challenges the traditional binary understanding of gender and opens up possibilities for more fluid and inclusive identities.

**bell hooks:** A prominent feminist thinker, hooks emphasizes the intersectionality of gender with race, class, and other forms of identity. In works like "Ain't I a Woman?" (1981), she critiques mainstream feminism for often ignoring the experiences of women of color and calls for a more inclusive and transformative approach to gender equality.

**Michel Foucault:** Foucault's work on power and knowledge offers valuable insights into how societal institutions shape and regulate gender norms. His analysis of how discourses around sexuality and the body are constructed helps us understand the mechanisms through which gender roles are enforced and challenged.

**Angela Davis:** As an activist and scholar, Davis has written extensively on the intersections of gender, race, and class. Her work highlights the importance of addressing systemic inequalities and advocates for a collective struggle towards social justice.

**Nancy Fraser:** Fraser's theory of social justice combines redistribution and recognition, arguing that addressing economic inequalities must go hand in hand with cultural and symbolic recognition of marginalized groups. Her work emphasizes the need for an integrated approach to gender equality.

## Gender Bias in Education and Workforce

**Educational Opportunities and Challenges:** Education is a cornerstone for achieving gender equality, providing individuals with the knowledge and skills to participate fully in society. While significant progress has been made in increasing access to education for girls and women, challenges remain.

**Access and Enrollment:** In many parts of the world, girls face barriers to accessing education, including poverty, cultural norms, and safety concerns. Initiatives such as scholarships, community awareness programs, and safe school environments are crucial for overcoming these barriers.

**Retention and Achievement:** Even when girls enroll in school, they may face challenges in staying and excelling. Factors such as early marriage, household responsibilities, and gender biases in teaching practices can impact their educational attainment. Efforts to create supportive learning environments and address specific needs are essential.

**STEM Education:** Encouraging girls to pursue STEM fields is vital for closing the gender gap in high-paying and influential careers. Programs that provide mentorship, role models, and hands-on learning experiences can help break down stereotypes and inspire more girls to enter these fields.

**Workplace Dynamics and Gender Equality:**

**Representation and Leadership:** Women remain underrepresented in leadership positions across various sectors. Initiatives such as leadership training, mentorship programs, and policies promoting work-life balance can help address this gap. Diverse leadership teams are shown to improve organizational performance and innovation.

**Pay Equity:** The gender pay gap persists, with women often earning less than men for the same work. Transparency in pay structures, regular audits, and advocating for equal pay can help address this issue. Additionally, recognizing and valuing traditionally female-dominated professions, such as caregiving and teaching, is crucial.

**Workplace Culture:** Creating an inclusive workplace culture that values diversity and challenges stereotypes is essential for achieving gender equality. This includes addressing issues such as harassment, discrimination, and bias in hiring and promotion practices. Training programs, clear policies, and a commitment to diversity can foster a more equitable environment.

**Work-Life Balance:** Policies such as parental leave, flexible working hours, and affordable childcare support both men and women in balancing work and family responsibilities. Promoting a culture where both genders are encouraged to take on caregiving roles can help dismantle traditional norms and support gender equality.

## Insights from Thought Leaders on Gender in Professional Environments

**Sheryl Sandberg:** In her book "Lean In" (2013), Sandberg discusses the challenges women face in the workplace and encourages women to assert themselves and pursue leadership roles. She advocates for systemic changes and personal strategies to support women's advancement.

**Ruth Bader Ginsburg:** As a Supreme Court Justice, Ginsburg's work and legal decisions have been instrumental in advancing gender equality. Her advocacy for equal rights and her own career serve as powerful examples of challenging and overcoming gender biases.

**Emma Watson:** An advocate for gender equality, Watson's work with the United Nations

HeForShe campaign highlights the importance of involving men in the fight for gender equality. Her speeches and activism emphasize that gender equality benefits everyone and requires collective effort.

**Gloria Steinem:** A leading figure in the feminist movement, Steinem's work has spanned decades of advocacy for women's rights. Her writings and activism continue to inspire and educate on issues of gender equality and social justice.

**Malala Yousafzai:** As an advocate for girls' education, Malala's story and work highlight the transformative power of education in challenging gender norms and empowering individuals. Her courage and activism have brought global attention to the importance of education for all.

## Conclusion: Moving Towards Gender Equality in Education and Workforce

Addressing gender bias in education and the workforce is a complex and ongoing process that requires commitment and action from individuals, organizations, and governments. By implementing policies that promote equality, raising awareness about biases, and creating supportive environments, we can work towards a more inclusive and equitable society.

Education is a powerful tool for challenging gender norms and empowering individuals, while a fair and inclusive workplace is essential for achieving gender equality. By addressing the unique challenges faced by both genders and promoting strategies that support equality, we can create a society where everyone has the opportunity to thrive.

The insights from thought leaders and the strategies outlined in this chapter provide valuable guidance for achieving gender equality. It's essential to recognize that this is not merely a women's issue or a men's issue, but a societal issue that affects everyone. Gender equality leads to diverse and inclusive environments where different perspectives and ideas can flourish, ultimately benefiting communities, organizations, and economies.

**Key Steps Forward:**

1. **Continued Advocacy and Policy Reform:** Governments and organizations must continue to advocate for and implement policies that support gender equality. This includes not only addressing overt discrimination but also tackling more subtle forms of bias and structural inequalities that perpetuate gender disparities.

2. **Education and Training:** Ongoing education and training on gender sensitivity and inclusion are crucial. This involves integrating gender equality into educational curricula, providing professional development for educators and leaders, and fostering environments where critical discussions about gender can take place.

3. **Empowerment and Mentorship:** Creating opportunities for mentorship and empowerment can help individuals overcome barriers and advance in their educational and professional journeys. Mentorship programs, leadership development initiatives, and networks of support are key components of this effort.

4. **Cultural Change:** Promoting a cultural shift towards valuing diversity and inclusion is fundamental. This requires challenging and changing entrenched stereotypes and norms, celebrating diverse representations of gender, and creating environments where all individuals feel valued and supported.

5. **Collective Responsibility:** Achieving gender equality is a collective responsibility that requires the participation of all members of society. Men and boys, as well as women and girls, must be engaged in efforts to promote

equality and challenge harmful norms and practices.

6. **Measurement and Accountability:** Regularly measuring progress and holding individuals and organizations accountable for their commitments to gender equality are essential. This includes conducting audits, setting measurable goals, and transparently reporting on outcomes.

In conclusion, moving towards gender equality in education and the workforce is not only a matter of justice but also a catalyst for broader social and economic progress. By embracing the principles of equality and inclusion, we can create a world where everyone has the opportunity to realize their full potential, contributing to a richer, more vibrant, and more equitable society for all.

# Chapter Three

# Gender Bias in Education and Workforce

## Educational Opportunities and Challenges for Both Genders

Education is a fundamental right and a powerful tool for achieving gender equality. It provides individuals with the knowledge and skills necessary to participate fully in society and is critical for personal and societal development. Despite significant progress in many parts of the world, gender biases in education persist, affecting both boys and girls, albeit in different ways.

**Access and Enrollment:**

Globally, access to education has improved considerably, with higher enrollment rates for both boys and girls. However, disparities remain. In some regions, particularly in low-income and conflict-affected areas, girls still face significant barriers to accessing education. These barriers include poverty, cultural norms favoring boys' education, early marriage, and safety concerns.

**Retention and Achievement:**

While enrollment rates have increased, retaining students and ensuring they complete their education remains a challenge. Girls are more likely to drop out due to factors such as household responsibilities, early marriage, and gender-based violence. Boys, on the other hand, may leave school to work and support their families, particularly in economically disadvantaged areas. Addressing these issues requires targeted interventions to support both genders, such as providing scholarships, improving school infrastructure, and promoting community awareness about the importance of education.

**Curriculum and Teaching Practices:**

Gender biases can also be found in the content of educational materials and teaching practices. Textbooks often portray stereotypical gender roles, with men depicted in active, professional roles and women in passive, domestic ones. This can reinforce traditional gender norms and limit students' aspirations. Efforts to revise curricula and incorporate gender-sensitive teaching practices are essential for promoting gender equality in education. Teachers play a crucial role in this process, and providing them with training on gender sensitivity can help create a more inclusive learning environment.

**STEM Education:**

Science, Technology, Engineering, and Mathematics (STEM) fields have historically been male-dominated. Encouraging girls to pursue STEM education is crucial for closing the gender gap in these high-paying and influential careers. Initiatives such as mentorship programs, role models, and hands-on learning experiences can inspire more girls to enter STEM fields. Additionally, addressing stereotypes and biases that suggest boys are naturally better at STEM subjects is vital for fostering an inclusive environment.

## Workplace Dynamics and Gender Equality

Gender bias in the workforce is a pervasive issue that affects career opportunities, earnings, and job satisfaction for both men and women. Addressing these biases requires a comprehensive understanding of how they manifest and targeted strategies to promote equality.

**Representation and Leadership:**

Women remain underrepresented in leadership positions across various sectors, including business, politics, academia, and technology. This underrepresentation is often referred to as the "glass ceiling," a metaphor for the invisible barriers that prevent women from advancing to top positions. Several factors contribute to this phenomenon, including gender stereotypes, biased recruitment and promotion practices, and work-life balance challenges.

Promoting gender diversity in leadership involves implementing policies such as leadership training programs, mentorship opportunities, and initiatives to encourage work-life balance. Organizations can also adopt transparent promotion criteria and actively work to identify and address biases in recruitment and evaluation processes. Diverse leadership teams have been shown to improve organizational performance and foster innovation, making gender diversity a strategic advantage.

**Pay Equity:**

The gender pay gap remains a significant issue, with women often earning less than men for the same work. This gap can be attributed to various factors, including occupational segregation, differences in work experience, and discrimination. Addressing pay equity requires a multifaceted approach, including conducting regular pay audits, implementing transparent pay structures, and advocating for equal pay for equal work.

Policies such as pay transparency, where employees have access to information about salary ranges and criteria for pay increases, can help reduce the gender pay gap. Additionally, recognizing and valuing traditionally female-dominated professions, such as caregiving and teaching, is crucial for promoting pay equity.

**Workplace Culture:**

Creating an inclusive workplace culture that values diversity and challenges stereotypes is essential for achieving gender equality. This involves addressing issues such as harassment, discrimination, and bias in hiring and promotion practices. Training programs on diversity and inclusion, clear anti-harassment policies, and a commitment to fostering a respectful and supportive work environment are critical components of an inclusive workplace culture.

Organizations can also implement employee resource groups (ERGs) that provide support and networking opportunities for underrepresented groups. ERGs can play a vital role in advocating for inclusive policies and practices and promoting a sense of belonging among employees.

**Work-Life Balance:**

Balancing work and family responsibilities is a challenge that affects both men and women, although societal expectations often place a greater burden on women. Policies such as parental leave, flexible working hours, and affordable childcare support employees in managing their work and family commitments. Encouraging a culture where both genders are supported and expected to take on caregiving roles can help dismantle traditional norms and promote gender equality.

Parental leave policies that offer equal leave for both mothers and fathers are particularly important for challenging gender norms around caregiving. When men are encouraged and supported in taking parental leave, it helps normalize the idea that caregiving is a shared responsibility, benefiting both families and workplaces.


## Insights from Thought Leaders on Gender in Professional Environments

Sheryl Sandberg:

In her book "Lean In" (2013), Sheryl Sandberg discusses the challenges women face in the workplace and encourages women to assert themselves and pursue leadership roles. She emphasizes the importance of mentorship, advocating for oneself, and addressing internal barriers, such as self-doubt and fear of failure.

Sandberg also highlights the role of organizations in creating supportive environments that enable women to thrive.

**Ruth Bader Ginsburg:**

As a Supreme Court Justice, Ruth Bader Ginsburg's work and legal decisions have been instrumental in advancing gender equality. Her advocacy for equal rights and her own career serve as powerful examples of challenging and overcoming gender biases. Ginsburg's legal opinions and public speeches often emphasized the importance of dismantling systemic barriers and ensuring equal opportunities for all genders.

**Emma Watson:**

An advocate for gender equality, Emma Watson's work with the United Nations HeForShe campaign highlights the importance of involving men in the fight for gender equality. Her speeches and activism emphasize that gender equality benefits everyone and requires collective effort. Watson advocates for inclusive policies and practices that support both men and women in achieving their full potential.

**Gloria Steinem:**

A leading figure in the feminist movement, Gloria Steinem's work has spanned decades of advocacy for women's rights. Her writings and activism continue to inspire and educate on issues of gender equality and social justice. Steinem emphasizes the importance of intersectionality, recognizing that gender biases are intertwined with other forms of discrimination, such as race, class, and sexuality.

**Malala Yousafzai:**

As an advocate for girls' education, Malala Yousafzai's story and work highlight the transformative power of education in challenging gender norms and empowering individuals. Her courage and activism have brought global attention to the importance of education for all and have inspired countless individuals to advocate for gender equality in their own communities.

## Strategies for Achieving Gender Balance in Education and Workforce

Achieving gender balance in education and the workforce requires a comprehensive and multi-faceted approach. Here are some strategies that can help promote gender equality:

### 1. Policy Interventions:

Governments and organizations can implement policies that promote gender equality, such as:

- Enacting laws that guarantee equal pay for equal work.

- Providing parental leave and flexible working arrangements.

- Ensuring access to affordable childcare.

- Implementing quotas or targets for gender representation in leadership positions.

## 2. Education and Awareness:

Raising awareness about gender biases and promoting gender-sensitive education are crucial steps in achieving gender equality. This can include:

- Revising curricula to include diverse and non-stereotypical representations of genders.

- Providing gender sensitivity training for teachers and educators.

- Encouraging critical thinking and discussions about gender norms and stereotypes in classrooms.

## 3. Mentorship and Support:

Mentorship programs and support networks can help individuals navigate gender biases and advance in their careers. Organizations can:

- Establish mentorship programs that connect junior employees with experienced mentors.

- Create employee resource groups (ERGs) that provide support and advocacy for underrepresented groups.

- Offer leadership training and development programs for women and other underrepresented groups.

## 4. Addressing Workplace Culture:

Creating an inclusive workplace culture is essential for promoting gender equality. This involves:

- Implementing diversity and inclusion training programs.

- Establishing clear anti-harassment and anti-discrimination policies.

- Promoting a culture of respect and support, where all employees feel valued and included.

## 5. Promoting Work-Life Balance:

Supporting employees in balancing work and family responsibilities is crucial for achieving gender equality. Organizations can:

- Offer flexible working hours and remote work options.

- Provide parental leave and encourage both mothers and fathers to take advantage of it.

- Ensure access to affordable and high-quality childcare services.

## 6. Challenging Stereotypes:

Challenging and changing gender stereotypes is a critical step in achieving gender equality. This can be done by:

- Promoting positive and diverse representations of genders in media and advertising.

- Encouraging individuals to question and challenge traditional gender norms.

- Supporting initiatives and campaigns that raise awareness about gender biases and promote equality.

## Conclusion: Moving Towards Gender Equality in Education and Workforce

Addressing gender bias in education and the workforce is a complex and ongoing process that requires commitment and action from individuals, organizations, and governments. By implementing policies that promote equality, raising awareness about biases, and creating supportive environments, we can work towards a more inclusive and equitable society.

Education is a powerful tool for challenging gender norms and empowering individuals, while a fair and inclusive workplace is essential for achieving gender equality. By addressing the unique challenges faced by both genders and promoting strategies that support equality, we can create a society where everyone has the opportunity to thrive.

The insights from thought leaders and the strategies outlined in this chapter provide valuable guidance for achieving gender equality. It's essential to recognize that this is not merely a women's issue or a men's issue, but a societal issue that affects everyone. Gender equality leads to diverse and inclusive environments where different perspectives and ideas can flourish, ultimately benefiting communities, organizations, and economies.

**Key Steps Forward:**

1. **Continued Advocacy and Policy Reform:** Governments and organizations must continue to advocate for and implement policies that support

gender equality. This includes not only addressing overt discrimination but also tackling more subtle forms of bias and structural inequalities that perpetuate gender disparities.

2. **Education and Training:** Ongoing education and training on gender sensitivity and inclusion are crucial. This involves integrating gender equality into educational curricula, providing professional development for educators and leaders, and fostering environments where critical discussions about gender can take place.

3. **Empowerment and Mentorship:** Creating opportunities for mentorship and empowerment can help individuals overcome barriers and advance in their educational and professional journeys. Mentorship programs, leadership development initiatives, and networks of support are key components of this effort.

4. **Cultural Change:** Promoting a cultural shift towards valuing diversity and inclusion is fundamental. This requires challenging and changing entrenched stereotypes and norms, celebrating diverse representations of gender, and creating environments where all individuals feel valued and supported.

5. **Collective Responsibility:** Achieving gender equality is a collective responsibility that requires the participation of all members of society. Men and boys, as well as women and girls, must be engaged in efforts to promote equality and challenge harmful norms and practices.

6. **Measurement and Accountability:** Regularly measuring progress and holding individuals and organizations accountable for their commitments to gender equality are essential. This includes conducting audits, setting measurable goals, and transparently reporting on outcomes.

In conclusion, moving towards gender equality in education and the workforce is not only a matter of justice but also a catalyst for broader social and economic progress. By embracing the principles of equality and inclusion, we can create a world where everyone has the opportunity to realize their full potential, contributing to a richer, more vibrant, and more equitable society for all.

# Chapter Four

# Media, Culture, and Gender Stereotypes



## The Influence of Media on Gender Perceptions

Media plays a pivotal role in shaping societal norms and perceptions, including those related to gender. From advertising and films to news media and social media platforms, the portrayal of men and women often reinforces existing stereotypes and expectations. Understanding the impact of media on gender stereotypes is crucial for promoting more equitable representations and challenging harmful narratives.

## Historical Perspectives:

Throughout history, media representations of gender have reflected and reinforced prevailing social norms. Early media, such as print advertisements and films from the mid-20th century, often depicted women in domestic roles, emphasizing beauty and homemaking skills. Men, meanwhile, were typically portrayed as breadwinners and leaders, reinforcing notions of masculinity tied to power and authority.

The advent of television and later digital media expanded the reach and influence of these stereotypes. Television shows and movies continued to depict gender in limited and often stereotypical ways, perpetuating narrow ideals of femininity and masculinity. Even as media evolved, these portrayals persisted, shaping how individuals perceive themselves and others.

**Contemporary Media Landscape:**

In the 21st century, media representations of gender have become more diverse yet still fraught with stereotypes and biases. While there have been strides towards more inclusive and nuanced portrayals, challenges remain in challenging deeply ingrained norms and addressing intersectional identities.

**Advertising and Consumer Culture:**

Advertising is a powerful force in shaping consumer behavior and societal norms. Advertisements often reinforce traditional gender roles, portraying women as caregivers and objects of beauty, and men as strong and assertive. These depictions not only influence purchasing decisions but also contribute to broader perceptions of gender roles and expectations.

Critics argue that advertising perpetuates harmful stereotypes, such as the objectification of women's bodies or the portrayal of men as emotionally distant. However, some advertisers have begun to challenge these norms by featuring diverse and empowered representations of gender. Campaigns promoting body positivity, gender-neutral products, and inclusivity reflect changing attitudes towards gender in consumer culture.

**Representation in Film and Television:**

Film and television are influential mediums for storytelling and cultural expression. While there have been notable successes in diversifying gender representations, stereotypes persist in mainstream media. Women are often portrayed in supporting or stereotypical roles, while men dominate leading and action-oriented roles. The underrepresentation of women, people of color, LGBTQ+ individuals, and other marginalized groups remains a significant issue.

Recent movements like MeToo and OscarsSoWhite have brought attention to the lack of diversity and equity in Hollywood and beyond. These movements have sparked conversations about systemic inequalities and the need for greater representation and inclusivity in media production and storytelling.

**Social Media and Digital Platforms:**

The rise of social media has democratized content creation and distribution, providing platforms for diverse voices and perspectives. However, social media can also amplify existing gender stereotypes and create new challenges. Influencers and celebrities often promote idealized images of beauty and success, perpetuating unrealistic expectations for both men and women.

Moreover, social media can be a space for harassment and cyberbullying based on gender identity and expression. Women, in particular, may face threats and abuse online, highlighting the intersection between digital culture and gender-based violence. Addressing these challenges requires robust policies, digital literacy initiatives, and community-based efforts to promote respectful and inclusive online interactions.

## Cultural Influences on Gender Stereotypes

Culture plays a significant role in shaping attitudes towards gender, with norms varying widely across societies and historical contexts. Understanding cultural influences on gender stereotypes can provide insights into how these norms are constructed, maintained, and challenged.

**Cross-Cultural Perspectives:**

Gender norms and expectations vary across cultures, reflecting unique histories, traditions, and belief systems. In some cultures, there are strict divisions of labor based on gender, with women primarily responsible for caregiving and domestic duties, while men are expected to provide for their families economically. These divisions can limit opportunities for both genders to pursue education, careers, and leadership roles.

Conversely, some cultures have more fluid or egalitarian views of gender, recognizing a spectrum of identities and roles beyond traditional binaries. Indigenous cultures, for example, may have long-standing traditions of gender diversity and acceptance, challenging Western notions of gender norms and roles.

**Religious and Ethical Perspectives:**

Religious beliefs and ethical frameworks also shape attitudes towards gender and sexuality. Many religious traditions have specific teachings on gender roles, marriage, and family life, influencing cultural practices and social norms. These teachings can be both supportive and restrictive, depending on interpretations and contexts.

In recent years, religious and ethical leaders have engaged in dialogues about gender equality and LGBTQ+ rights, advocating for inclusive interpretations and practices. These conversations are essential for fostering understanding and respect for diverse gender identities and expressions within religious and cultural communities.

**Media and Cultural Hegemony:**

Media often reflects and reinforces cultural hegemony, where dominant ideologies and values are promoted as natural and inevitable. In many societies, media representations of gender align with prevailing cultural norms, reinforcing stereotypes and expectations. This can create challenges for individuals and groups who do not conform to these norms, leading to marginalization and discrimination.

Critically analyzing media and cultural representations of gender is essential for challenging hegemonic norms and promoting social change. By amplifying diverse voices and narratives, media can play a transformative role in shifting attitudes towards gender equality and inclusivity.

## Philosophical Insights on Gender Stereotypes

Philosophers and scholars offer critical perspectives on the nature and impact of gender stereotypes, challenging us to rethink assumptions and promote social justice.

**Judith Butler:** Butler's theory of gender performativity argues that gender is not a fixed identity but a social construct performed through repeated actions and behaviors. This perspective challenges essentialist views of gender and opens up possibilities for understanding gender as fluid and socially constructed.

**Simone de Beauvoir:** In "The Second Sex" (1949), de Beauvoir explores the ways in which women are defined and oppressed by patriarchal society. Her analysis of gender as a social construction influenced feminist theory and activism, highlighting the need to dismantle stereotypes and promote women's autonomy and equality.

**bell hooks:** hooks' intersectional feminism critiques the intersections of race, class, and gender in shaping identity and oppression. In works like "Feminist Theory: From Margin to Center" (1984), she argues for a feminism that is inclusive of diverse experiences and perspectives, challenging dominant narratives and promoting social justice.

**Michel Foucault:** Foucault's analysis of power and discourse offers insights into how gender stereotypes are produced and maintained through societal institutions and practices. His work encourages critical reflection on the ways in which power operates to regulate and normalize gender identities and behaviors.

**Nancy Fraser:** Fraser's theory of recognition emphasizes the importance of affirming and valuing marginalized identities, including gender identities. She argues that achieving gender justice requires both redistributive measures to address material inequalities and recognition of the cultural and symbolic dimensions of oppression.

## Strategies for Challenging Gender Stereotypes in Media and Culture

Addressing gender stereotypes in media and culture requires a multifaceted approach that combines policy interventions, media literacy, cultural activism, and community engagement. Here are some strategies for promoting more equitable representations:

### 1. Policy and Regulation:

Governments and regulatory bodies can enact policies that promote diversity and inclusivity in media content. This includes:

- Implementing guidelines for gender-sensitive advertising and media production.

- Supporting initiatives that promote diverse representation both on-screen and behind the scenes.

- Enforcing regulations against harmful and discriminatory content that perpetuates stereotypes.

## 2. Media Literacy and Education:

Promoting media literacy is crucial for empowering individuals to critically analyze and challenge gender stereotypes in media. Educational institutions can integrate media literacy into curricula, teaching students to deconstruct media messages and understand their impact on attitudes and behaviors.

Community-based media literacy programs can also engage diverse audiences in conversations about gender representation and encourage media producers to adopt more inclusive practices.

## 3. Promoting Diverse Voices and Narratives:

Supporting diverse creators and storytellers is essential for promoting authentic and inclusive representations of gender. Media organizations can:

- Fund projects that amplify marginalized voices and experiences.

- Provide platforms for diverse content creators to share their stories and perspectives.

- Foster partnerships with community organizations and grassroots initiatives that promote cultural diversity and social justice.

## 4. Cultural and Community Engagement:

Engaging with cultural and community leaders can foster dialogue and collaboration on challenging gender stereotypes. Religious and ethical leaders, educators, artists, and activists can work together to promote positive representations of gender and advocate for social change.

Community-based initiatives, such as film festivals, art exhibitions, and public forums, can create spaces for discussing gender issues and showcasing alternative narratives that challenge stereotypes.

## 5. Corporate Responsibility and Accountability:

Media companies and advertisers have a responsibility to promote ethical and inclusive representations of gender. Corporate policies and practices can:

- Establish diversity and inclusion initiatives that prioritize gender equity.

- Conduct regular audits and assessments to monitor progress towards diversity goals.

- Partner with advocacy organizations and experts to develop best practices for inclusive media content.

**6. Empowering Audiences and Consumers:**

Empowering audiences and consumers to demand more diverse and inclusive media content is essential for driving change. Campaigns, boycotts, and social media movements can mobilize public opinion and pressure media companies to adopt more progressive policies and practices.

By collectively advocating for media representation that reflects the diversity of human experiences, we can challenge gender stereotypes, promote social justice, and create a more inclusive society for all.

## Conclusion: Promoting Gender Equality Through Media and Cultural Change

Media and culture are powerful forces that shape how we perceive ourselves and others, including our understanding of gender. By challenging stereotypes, promoting diverse representations, and fostering critical engagement, we can create media and cultural environments that support gender equality and social justice.

The insights from this chapter underscore the importance of addressing gender stereotypes in media and culture as part of broader efforts towards equality. By amplifying diverse voices, challenging dominant narratives, and advocating for inclusive practices, we can create a more equitable society where everyone's experiences and identities are respected and valued.

**Key Strategies Moving Forward:**

1. **Advocacy and Awareness:** Continued advocacy efforts are essential for raising awareness about the impact of media on gender perceptions. By engaging with policymakers, media professionals, and the public, we can promote policies and practices that prioritize diversity and representation.

2. **Education and Empowerment:** Media literacy programs and educational initiatives play a crucial role in empowering individuals to critically analyze media messages and challenge stereotypes. By equipping people with the tools to deconstruct and reinterpret media narratives, we can promote more nuanced understandings of gender and identity.

3. **Collaboration and Community Engagement:** Building partnerships between media creators, cultural institutions, and community organizations can amplify diverse voices and promote inclusive storytelling. By collaborating on projects that reflect the richness of human experiences, we can foster empathy, understanding, and social cohesion.

4. **Corporate Responsibility:** Media companies and advertisers have a responsibility to prioritize ethical and inclusive representations of gender. By adopting diversity policies, conducting regular audits, and engaging with stakeholders, companies can contribute to positive social change and build trust with audiences.

5. **Cultural Shifts:** Promoting cultural shifts towards gender equality involves challenging ingrained norms and behaviors that perpetuate

discrimination. By celebrating diverse identities and challenging stereotypes in everyday interactions, we can create more inclusive environments where everyone can thrive.

In conclusion, promoting gender equality through media and cultural change requires collective action and a commitment to challenging inequality at all levels of society. By harnessing the power of media and culture to promote diversity, representation, and social justice, we can create a future where everyone has the opportunity to live free from discrimination and fulfill their potential.

Through ongoing dialogue, advocacy, and creative expression, we can pave the way for a more equitable world where diverse gender identities and experiences are celebrated and respected. Together, we can shape a future where media and culture serve as catalysts for positive social change and equality for all.

# Chapter Five

# Gender and Emotional Well-being

<u>Understanding Emotional Well-being Across Gender</u>

Emotional well-being encompasses an individual's ability to cope with stress, maintain positive relationships, and achieve a sense of fulfillment in life. Gender plays a significant role in shaping emotional experiences and responses, influenced by societal expectations, biological factors, and individual experiences. This chapter explores the complexities of gender and emotional well-being, highlighting key factors that impact mental health and offering insights into promoting emotional resilience and support for individuals of all genders.

**Biological and Psychosocial Influences:**

Biological differences between genders, such as hormonal fluctuations and brain structure, can influence emotional experiences and responses. For instance, research suggests that hormonal variations, particularly during puberty and menopause, may contribute to mood disorders such as depression and anxiety, which affect individuals differently based on gender.

Psychosocial factors, including societal norms and cultural expectations, also play a crucial role in shaping emotional well-being. Stereotypical expectations of masculinity and femininity can impact how individuals express and perceive emotions, influencing their mental health outcomes. Societal pressures to conform to rigid gender roles can contribute to stress, anxiety, and feelings of inadequacy among both men and women.

**Gender Differences in Emotional Expression:**

Traditional gender norms often prescribe specific ways of expressing emotions. Men are frequently socialized to suppress vulnerability and display traits of stoicism and emotional strength, while women may be encouraged to express empathy and nurturing behaviors. These norms can create barriers to authentic emotional expression and contribute to mental health challenges.

Research indicates that societal expectations of emotional restraint among men can lead to higher rates of depression and substance abuse. Conversely, women may face challenges related to emotional labor, balancing caregiving responsibilities with their own well-being. Understanding these gendered dynamics is essential for developing interventions that support healthy emotional expression and resilience.

**Intersectionality and Multiple Identities:**

Intersectionality recognizes that individuals hold multiple identities that intersect and influence their experiences of gender and emotional well-being. Factors such as race, ethnicity, sexual orientation, socioeconomic status, and disability can intersect with gender to shape mental health outcomes and access to support services.

Marginalized groups, such as transgender individuals and people of color, often face compounded stigma and discrimination that impact their emotional well-being. Intersectional approaches to mental health care are critical for addressing these unique challenges and promoting inclusive practices that honor diverse identities and experiences.

**Impact of Trauma and Adversity:**

Experiences of trauma and adversity, including violence, discrimination, and systemic oppression, can profoundly impact emotional well-being across genders. Women and gender minorities, in particular, may experience higher rates of trauma related to gender-based violence and discrimination, leading to increased risk of depression, PTSD, and other mental health disorders.

Men, while less likely to seek help for emotional distress, may experience trauma related to societal pressures to conform to masculine norms of strength and self-reliance. Addressing the impact of trauma requires trauma-informed approaches that recognize and validate individuals' experiences while providing supportive interventions tailored to their needs.

**Mental Health Disorders and Gender:**

Gender differences exist in the prevalence and presentation of mental health disorders. For example, women are more likely to be diagnosed with mood disorders such as depression and anxiety, whereas men may exhibit externalizing behaviors associated with conditions like ADHD and conduct disorder. These differences reflect complex interactions between biological, psychological, and social factors.

Stigma surrounding mental illness can also vary by gender, influencing help-seeking behaviors and treatment outcomes. Men, in particular, may face stigma related to admitting vulnerability or seeking psychological support, contributing to underdiagnosis and undertreatment of mental health conditions.

**Promoting Emotional Resilience and Support:**

Enhancing emotional resilience involves fostering adaptive coping strategies and supportive environments that promote well-being across genders. Key strategies include:

- **Promoting Emotional Literacy:** Educating individuals about emotions and promoting skills for identifying, expressing, and regulating feelings can enhance emotional intelligence and resilience.

- **Encouraging Help-Seeking Behaviors:** Normalizing help-seeking behaviors and reducing stigma associated with mental health care can encourage individuals to seek timely support when needed.

- **Building Supportive Communities:** Creating inclusive spaces that validate diverse emotional experiences and provide social support can enhance well-being and reduce isolation.

- **Addressing Systemic Inequities:** Advocating for policies and practices that address systemic inequities, such as access to affordable healthcare and social services, can promote equitable mental health outcomes for all genders.

## Cultural Perspectives on Emotional Well-being:

Cultural beliefs and practices influence how emotional well-being is understood and addressed within communities. For example, some cultures prioritize collective well-being over individual distress, emphasizing community support and spiritual healing practices. Understanding cultural perspectives can inform culturally responsive approaches to mental health care that respect and integrate diverse beliefs and values.

## Philosophical Insights on Emotions:

Philosophers have long debated the nature and significance of emotions, offering insights into how emotions shape human experiences and ethical frameworks. For example:

- **Aristotle** viewed emotions as integral to moral virtue, emphasizing the importance of cultivating balanced emotional responses.

- **Spinoza** explored the relationship between emotions and rationality, arguing for understanding and managing emotions through reason.

- **Nietzsche** challenged conventional views of emotions, celebrating their creative and transformative potential in personal and social life.

- **Existentialist thinkers**, such as **Sartre** and **De Beauvoir**, examined the existential dimensions of emotions, exploring how emotions reflect individual freedom and responsibility.

## Strategies for Promoting Gender-Inclusive Emotional Well-being

Achieving gender-inclusive emotional well-being requires systemic changes and individual actions that prioritize mental health and resilience across genders. Here are key strategies for promoting gender-inclusive emotional well-being:

### 1. Education and Awareness:

Educating individuals and communities about the impact of gender norms on emotional health can promote empathy, understanding, and supportive relationships. This includes providing resources on emotional literacy, stress management, and mental health awareness tailored to diverse gender identities.

## 2. Accessible Mental Health Services:

Increasing access to culturally competent and inclusive mental health services is essential for addressing the unique needs of diverse gender identities. This involves training healthcare providers on gender-affirming practices, reducing barriers to care, and advocating for policies that prioritize mental health equity.

## 3. Intersectional Approaches:

Implementing intersectional approaches to mental health care acknowledges and addresses the compounded impact of multiple identities on emotional well-being. This includes providing specialized support for marginalized groups, such as transgender individuals and people of color, who experience intersecting forms of stigma and discrimination.

## 4. Promoting Positive Masculinities:

Challenging rigid norms of masculinity that discourage emotional expression and help-seeking behaviors is crucial for promoting mental health among men. Promoting positive role models and community initiatives that celebrate diverse expressions of masculinity can empower men to prioritize their emotional well-being.

## 5. Community Support and Advocacy:

Building supportive communities that foster belonging, validation, and social connection can enhance emotional resilience and reduce isolation. Community-based organizations, support groups, and peer networks play a vital role in promoting peer support and advocacy for gender-inclusive mental health policies.

## 6. Research and Policy Reform:

Investing in research on gender and emotional well-being can inform evidence-based policies and practices that promote equitable mental health outcomes. Advocating for policy reform, funding mental health initiatives, and integrating gender-sensitive approaches into public health strategies are critical steps towards achieving systemic change.

## Conclusion: Towards Gender-Inclusive Emotional Well-being

Gender plays a significant role in shaping emotional experiences and responses, influenced by biological, social, and cultural factors. By understanding the complexities of gender and emotional well-being and addressing systemic barriers to mental health care, we can promote resilience, support, and equity across genders.

Through education, advocacy, and community engagement, we can challenge stereotypes, empower individuals, and create environments where everyone can thrive emotionally. By promoting inclusive practices, supporting diverse identities, and prioritizing mental health equity, we move closer to a future where emotional well-being is valued, protected, and supported for all individuals, regardless of gender.

# Chapter Six

# Legal and Policy Frameworks

<u>Introduction to Gender Equality Legislation</u>

Legal and policy frameworks play a crucial role in promoting gender equality and addressing discrimination. These frameworks establish the rights and protections necessary to ensure that all individuals, regardless of gender, have equal opportunities and are free from bias and violence. This chapter explores the evolution of gender equality laws, the impact of international treaties and conventions, and the challenges and opportunities in implementing effective legal and policy measures.

## Historical Evolution of Gender Equality Legislation

The fight for gender equality has a long and complex history, marked by significant milestones and ongoing struggles. Early efforts to secure gender equality focused primarily on women's suffrage and access to education and employment. Over time, these efforts expanded to address broader issues of discrimination and violence, leading to the development of comprehensive legal and policy frameworks.

- **Early Advocacy and Women's Suffrage:** The 19th and early 20th centuries saw significant movements for women's suffrage, leading to the right to vote for women in many countries. This period also witnessed early advocacy for women's rights to education and employment, laying the foundation for future gender equality legislation.

- **Post-War Advances and Human Rights:** The aftermath of World War II brought a renewed focus on human rights, with the adoption of the Universal Declaration of Human Rights in 1948. This period saw the establishment of international treaties and conventions aimed at protecting the rights of women and promoting gender equality.

- **Modern Legislation and Intersectionality:** In recent decades, gender equality legislation has increasingly recognized the importance of intersectionality, addressing the unique challenges faced by individuals at the intersections of gender, race, ethnicity, sexuality, and other identities. Modern legal frameworks aim to create comprehensive protections that reflect the diverse experiences of marginalized groups.

## International Treaties and Conventions

International treaties and conventions provide a crucial foundation for gender equality legislation, establishing global standards and commitments for protecting the rights of women and gender minorities. Key international instruments include:

- **Convention on the Elimination of All Forms of Discrimination Against Women (CEDAW):** Adopted by the United Nations in 1979, CEDAW is often referred to as the "bill of rights for women." It outlines comprehensive measures to eliminate discrimination against women in all areas of life, including education, employment, health, and political participation.

- Beijing Declaration and Platform for Action: The Fourth World Conference on Women, held in Beijing in 1995, produced a landmark declaration and platform for action, outlining strategic objectives and actions for achieving gender equality. The Beijing Platform for Action remains a key reference point for gender equality advocacy and policy development.

- **Sustainable Development Goals (SDGs):** The United Nations' 2030 Agenda for Sustainable Development includes specific goals and targets related to gender equality, particularly Goal 5: "Achieve gender equality and empower all women and girls." The SDGs provide a global framework for addressing gender disparities and promoting inclusive development.

- **International Labor Organization (ILO) Conventions:** The ILO has adopted several conventions that address gender equality in the workplace, including the Equal Remuneration Convention (1951) and the Discrimination (Employment and Occupation) Convention (1958). These conventions establish standards for equal pay, non-discrimination, and workplace protections.

## National Legislation and Policy Frameworks

National governments play a critical role in implementing gender equality legislation and policies that reflect international commitments and address local contexts. Key areas of focus include:

- **Equal Pay and Employment Protections:** Legislation that ensures equal pay for equal work and prohibits discrimination in hiring, promotion, and working conditions is essential for promoting gender equality in the workforce. Policies that support work-life balance, such as parental leave and flexible working arrangements, also contribute to gender equity.

- **Education and Health Rights:** Ensuring equal access to education and healthcare is fundamental for advancing gender equality. Policies that promote gender-sensitive curricula, address gender-based violence in schools, and provide comprehensive reproductive health services are crucial for empowering individuals and reducing disparities.

- **Political Participation and Leadership:** Legal frameworks that promote women's political participation and leadership are vital for achieving gender equality in decision-making processes. Measures such as gender quotas, campaign finance reforms, and support for women's political training can help increase women's representation in government and other leadership roles.

- **Violence Prevention and Support Services:** Addressing gender-based violence requires comprehensive legal protections and support services for survivors. Legislation that criminalizes domestic violence, sexual assault, and harassment, along with policies that provide accessible support services, is essential for ensuring safety and justice.

## Challenges in Implementing Gender Equality Legislation

Despite significant progress, numerous challenges remain in implementing effective gender equality legislation and policies. These challenges include:

- **Cultural and Social Norms:** Deeply entrenched cultural and social norms can hinder the implementation of gender equality laws. Efforts to change these norms through education, advocacy, and community engagement are critical for creating supportive environments for legal reforms.

- **Lack of Political Will:** Political resistance to gender equality reforms can impede progress. Building coalitions, raising public awareness, and engaging diverse stakeholders are strategies for generating political will and support for gender equality initiatives.

- **Resource Constraints**: Limited resources and funding can undermine the effectiveness of gender equality programs and services. Advocating for increased investment in gender equality and integrating gender considerations into budgeting processes are important for ensuring adequate support.

- **Intersectional Discrimination:** Addressing the unique challenges faced by individuals at the intersections of multiple identities requires comprehensive and inclusive legal frameworks. Ensuring that policies consider the diverse experiences of marginalized groups is essential for achieving true gender equality.

## Promising Practices and Innovations

Innovative approaches and promising practices from around the world offer valuable insights into advancing gender equality through legal and policy frameworks. Examples include:

- **Gender Budgeting:** Gender budgeting involves integrating gender perspectives into government budgets to ensure that resource allocation promotes gender equality. Countries such as Sweden and Rwanda have successfully implemented gender budgeting practices that have contributed to significant progress in gender equity.

- **Quota Systems:** Gender quotas for political representation have been effective in increasing women's participation in government. Countries like Norway and India have implemented quota systems that mandate a minimum percentage of women in legislative bodies, leading to greater gender diversity in decision-making processes.

- **Gender Mainstreaming:** Gender mainstreaming involves systematically incorporating gender considerations into all aspects of policy development, implementation, and evaluation. The European Union and other regions have adopted gender mainstreaming strategies to ensure that policies and programs promote gender equality.

- **Comprehensive Anti-Violence Legislation:** Countries such as Spain and Brazil have enacted comprehensive legislation to address gender-based violence, including measures for prevention, protection, and prosecution. These laws provide robust frameworks for supporting survivors and holding perpetrators accountable.

<u>**Philosophical and Ethical Perspectives on Gender Equality**</u>

Philosophical and ethical frameworks provide critical insights into the principles and values that underpin gender equality legislation. Key perspectives include:

- **Liberal Feminism:** Liberal feminism emphasizes individual rights and equal opportunities, advocating for legal reforms that promote gender equality in areas such as education, employment, and political participation.

- **Social Justice and Intersectionality:** Social justice frameworks highlight the importance of addressing systemic inequalities and recognizing the interconnectedness of various forms of discrimination. Intersectional approaches emphasize the need for inclusive policies that consider the diverse experiences of marginalized groups.

- **Human Rights and Dignity:** Human rights perspectives affirm the inherent dignity and worth of all individuals, advocating for legal protections that ensure equal rights and freedoms for people of all genders. This framework underpins many international treaties and conventions related to gender equality.

## The Role of Civil Society and Advocacy

Civil society organizations and advocacy groups play a vital role in advancing gender equality through legal and policy reforms. These organizations:

- **Advocate for Legal Reforms:** Civil society groups advocate for the adoption and implementation of gender equality laws, engaging with policymakers, raising public awareness, and mobilizing support for legislative initiatives.

- **Provide Support Services:** Many organizations offer essential support services for survivors of gender-based violence, including legal assistance, counseling, and shelter. These services are crucial for ensuring access to justice and support.

- **Monitor and Hold Governments Accountable:** Advocacy groups monitor the implementation of gender equality laws and policies, holding governments accountable for their commitments. This includes conducting research, publishing reports, and engaging in strategic litigation to address gaps and challenges.

## Conclusion: Advancing Gender Equality Through Legal and Policy Frameworks

Legal and policy frameworks are fundamental tools for promoting gender equality and addressing discrimination. While significant progress has been made, ongoing efforts are needed to overcome challenges and ensure the effective implementation of gender equality laws.

By drawing on international treaties, national legislation, and innovative practices, we can create comprehensive frameworks that promote equal opportunities and protections for individuals of all genders. Engaging diverse stakeholders, addressing intersectional discrimination, and fostering a supportive cultural environment are essential for achieving lasting change.

Ultimately, the pursuit of gender equality through legal and policy frameworks reflects our commitment to justice, dignity, and human rights for all. By continuing to advocate for and implement these frameworks, we can create a more equitable and inclusive society where everyone can thrive.

# Chapter Seven

# Gender Dynamics in Relationships



Gender dynamics in relationships are influenced by a complex interplay of societal norms, cultural expectations, and individual behaviors. These dynamics shape how partners interact, communicate, and support each other, impacting the overall quality and health of relationships. Understanding these influences is crucial for fostering equitable and fulfilling partnerships. This chapter delves into the various aspects of gender dynamics in relationships, examining historical perspectives, contemporary issues, and strategies for promoting gender equality and mutual respect.

## Historical Perspectives on Gender Roles in Relationships

Historically, gender roles in relationships have been defined by patriarchal structures that assigned men and women distinct and unequal roles. These roles were often rooted in the belief that men were natural leaders and providers, while women were caretakers and nurturers.

Such dynamics were reinforced through cultural narratives, legal frameworks, and social institutions.

- **Traditional Gender Roles:** In many societies, traditional gender roles dictated that men were the primary breadwinners and decision-makers, while women were expected to manage the household and care for children. This division of labor reinforced the notion of male dominance and female dependency within relationships.

- **Legal and Social Constraints:** Laws and social norms historically restricted women's rights and autonomy, limiting their ability to own property, work outside the home, or make independent decisions. These constraints further entrenched gender inequalities within relationships.

- **Changing Norms:** The feminist movements of the 20th century challenged traditional gender roles and advocated for greater equality and autonomy for women. These movements led to significant legal and social changes, including increased access to education and employment for women, as well as greater recognition of their rights within relationships.

# Contemporary Issues in Gender Dynamics

While significant progress has been made, contemporary relationships continue to be influenced by gender dynamics that reflect both traditional norms and modern challenges. Key issues include:

- **Balancing Career and Family:** Dual-career couples face the challenge of balancing professional aspirations with family responsibilities. Despite advances in gender equality, women often bear a disproportionate share of household and caregiving duties, leading to stress and potential conflicts.

- **Communication Styles:** Research indicates that men and women may have different communication styles, shaped by socialization and cultural expectations. These differences can lead to misunderstandings and conflicts if not addressed with empathy and mutual respect.

- **Power Dynamics:** Power imbalances within relationships can manifest in various ways, including financial control, decision-making authority, and emotional manipulation. These dynamics can undermine mutual respect and equality, leading to unhealthy and potentially abusive relationships.

- **Emotional Labor:** Women often perform a significant amount of emotional labor in relationships, managing not only their own emotions but also those of their partners and families. This invisible labor can contribute to emotional exhaustion and relationship strain.

- **Sexual Intimacy:** Gender dynamics also influence sexual relationships, with societal expectations and norms impacting sexual behavior, desires, and consent. Open communication and mutual respect are essential for fostering healthy and fulfilling sexual relationships.

## Intersectionality in Gender Dynamics

Understanding gender dynamics in relationships requires an intersectional approach that considers the impact of multiple identities and experiences. Factors such as race, ethnicity, sexual orientation, socioeconomic status, and disability intersect with gender to shape relationship dynamics in unique ways.

- **Race and Ethnicity:** Cultural beliefs and practices related to gender roles can vary significantly across different racial and ethnic communities. Understanding and respecting these cultural differences is important for promoting equity and inclusion within relationships.

- **Sexual Orientation:** Same-sex and queer relationships may challenge traditional gender norms in unique ways, offering alternative models of partnership and equality. However, these relationships can also face societal stigma and discrimination that impact their dynamics.

- **Socioeconomic Status:** Economic pressures and disparities can influence relationship dynamics, with financial stress impacting communication, power dynamics, and overall relationship satisfaction. Addressing economic inequalities is essential for promoting healthy and equitable relationships.

- **Disability:** Individuals with disabilities may face additional challenges in relationships, including societal stigma, accessibility issues, and the need for caregiving. Recognizing and addressing these challenges is crucial for fostering inclusive and supportive partnerships.

# Promoting Gender Equality in Relationships

Fostering gender equality in relationships involves challenging traditional norms, promoting open communication, and supporting mutual respect and collaboration. Key strategies include:

- **Communication and Empathy:** Open and honest communication is foundational for healthy relationships. Partners should strive to understand each other's perspectives, express their needs and emotions, and engage in active listening. Empathy and validation can help bridge communication gaps and build trust.

- **Shared Responsibilities:** Equitable division of household and caregiving responsibilities is essential for promoting balance and reducing stress. Partners should negotiate and share tasks based on mutual agreement and respect, recognizing the value of both paid and unpaid labor.

- **Financial Equality:** Financial transparency and equitable decision-making are crucial for preventing power imbalances. Partners should discuss financial goals, budgets, and responsibilities openly, ensuring that both have a say in financial matters.

- **Support for Personal Growth:** Supporting each other's personal and professional growth is important for maintaining a healthy and dynamic relationship. Partners should encourage each other's aspirations and provide emotional and practical support for achieving individual goals.

- **Addressing Power Imbalances:** Recognizing and addressing power imbalances requires ongoing reflection and action. Partners should be aware of how power dynamics manifest in their relationship and work together to ensure that both have an equal voice and agency.

- **Sexual Respect and Consent:** Healthy sexual relationships are built on mutual respect and consent. Partners should communicate openly about their desires and boundaries, ensuring that sexual interactions are consensual and satisfying for both.

## Cultural and Media Influences on Gender Dynamics

Cultural narratives and media representations play a significant role in shaping gender dynamics in relationships. These influences can reinforce stereotypes or challenge traditional norms, impacting how individuals perceive and navigate their partnerships.

- **Media Representations:** Media portrayals of relationships often reflect and perpetuate gender stereotypes, depicting men as dominant and women as submissive or nurturing. Challenging these representations and promoting diverse and realistic depictions of relationships is important for fostering healthy dynamics.

- **Cultural Narratives:** Cultural stories and traditions shape expectations of gender roles within relationships. While these narratives can provide valuable guidance and support, they can also limit individual expression and perpetuate inequalities. Critical engagement with cultural narratives can help individuals navigate their relationships in more equitable ways.

- **Education and Advocacy:** Educating individuals and communities about gender equality and healthy relationships is essential for challenging harmful norms and promoting positive dynamics. Advocacy efforts should aim to raise awareness, provide resources, and support policy changes that promote gender equity.

## Philosophical and Ethical Perspectives on Relationships

Philosophical and ethical frameworks offer valuable insights into the principles and values that underpin healthy and equitable relationships. Key perspectives include:

- **Feminist Ethics:** Feminist ethics emphasizes the importance of equality, care, and mutual respect within relationships. This framework challenges traditional power dynamics and advocates for partnerships based on shared responsibilities and support.

- **Virtue Ethics:** Virtue ethics focuses on the development of moral character and the cultivation of virtues such as empathy, honesty, and fairness. Applying virtue ethics to relationships encourages partners to strive for personal growth and moral excellence in their interactions.

- **Existentialist Perspectives:** Existentialist philosophers such as Jean-Paul Sartre and Simone de Beauvoir explore the nature of human freedom and responsibility in relationships. They emphasize the importance of authenticity, mutual recognition, and the ethical responsibility to support each other's freedom and well-being.

- **Relational Ethics:** Relational ethics highlights the interconnectedness of individuals and the ethical significance of relationships. This perspective emphasizes the importance of mutual care, respect, and interdependence in fostering ethical and fulfilling partnerships.

## Conclusion: Building Equitable and Fulfilling Relationships

Gender dynamics in relationships are shaped by a complex interplay of historical, cultural, and individual factors. While significant progress has been made in promoting gender equality, ongoing efforts are needed to address contemporary challenges and support equitable partnerships.

By fostering open communication, sharing responsibilities, addressing power imbalances, and promoting mutual respect, individuals can build healthy and fulfilling relationships. Understanding the impact of intersectionality and cultural influences is crucial for creating inclusive and supportive dynamics that honor diverse experiences and identities.

Philosophical and ethical perspectives offer valuable guidance for navigating the complexities of relationships, emphasizing the importance of equality, empathy, and mutual care. By applying these principles and advocating for broader social and cultural changes, we can create a future where relationships are defined by equity, respect, and mutual fulfillment for all individuals, regardless of gender.

# Chapter Eight

# The Role of Religion and Spirituality



## Introduction to Religion, Spirituality, and Gender Dynamics

Religion and spirituality have historically played significant roles in shaping societal norms, including those related to gender roles and relations. The teachings, practices, and interpretations of various religious traditions influence how gender is perceived and enacted within communities and individuals' lives. This chapter explores the complex interplay between religion, spirituality, and gender dynamics, examining both the ways in which religious beliefs have reinforced traditional gender roles and the potential for spiritual and religious frameworks to promote gender equality and liberation.

## Historical Perspectives on Religion and Gender Roles

Religious traditions have long been intertwined with societal structures, often reinforcing established gender roles and hierarchies.

Understanding the historical context of these influences provides insight into the contemporary challenges and opportunities for gender equality within religious and spiritual communities.

- **Patriarchal Interpretations:** Many of the world's major religions have historically been interpreted and practiced within patriarchal contexts, which have reinforced male dominance and female subordination. These interpretations have often been used to justify restrictive gender roles and limit women's rights and opportunities.

- **Sacred Texts and Gender Norms:** Sacred texts, such as the Bible, Quran, Torah, and others, contain passages that have been interpreted in ways that support traditional gender roles. For example, certain verses are cited to justify male authority in the family and religious institutions, as well as the exclusion of women from leadership roles.

- **Religious Institutions:** Religious institutions, such as churches, mosques, synagogues, and temples, have historically been male-dominated spaces. Leadership roles within these institutions have often been reserved for men, while women have been relegated to supportive or subordinate roles.

<u>**Contemporary Challenges and Opportunities**</u>

In the contemporary world, religious and spiritual beliefs continue to influence gender dynamics, both reinforcing traditional norms and providing frameworks for challenging and transforming them. Key areas of focus include:

- **Religious Teachings and Gender Equality:** Many religious communities are re-examining their teachings and traditions in light of contemporary understandings of gender equality. Progressive interpretations of sacred texts and doctrines are emerging, which advocate for the equal treatment and participation of women and men.

- **Women in Religious Leadership:** Increasingly, women are assuming leadership roles within religious institutions, challenging long-standing gender barriers. This shift is seen in various religious traditions, from women becoming priests and pastors in Christian denominations to female rabbis and Islamic scholars gaining prominence.

- **Spiritual Movements and Gender Liberation:** Spiritual movements that emphasize personal empowerment, social justice, and holistic well-being often advocate for gender equality. These movements draw on diverse spiritual traditions and practices to promote healing and liberation from oppressive gender norms.

- **Intersectionality in Religion and Spirituality:** Intersectional approaches recognize that religious and spiritual experiences are shaped by multiple identities, including race, ethnicity, class, and sexuality. Addressing these intersections is crucial for understanding and promoting gender equality within religious and spiritual contexts.

## Prominent Religious Traditions and Gender Perspectives

Examining the gender dynamics within major religious traditions provides a deeper understanding of the diverse ways in which religion and spirituality influence gender roles and equality.

- **Christianity:** Within Christianity, there is significant diversity in how gender roles are understood and practiced. While some denominations uphold traditional gender roles, others advocate for gender equality and ordain women as clergy. Feminist theology and liberation theology have been influential in promoting gender justice within Christian communities.

- **Islam:** In Islam, interpretations of gender roles vary widely across different cultural and theological contexts. While some interpretations support traditional roles, others advocate for gender equality based on principles of justice and mutual respect found in the Quran and Hadith. Islamic feminism seeks to reinterpret Islamic texts to support women's rights and empowerment.

- **Judaism:** Judaism encompasses a range of beliefs and practices regarding gender roles, from traditional Orthodox views to progressive Reform and Conservative movements that support gender equality. Feminist interpretations of Jewish texts and rituals aim to create more inclusive and egalitarian communities.

- **Hinduism:** Hinduism's diverse traditions and practices offer multiple perspectives on gender. While some texts and rituals uphold traditional gender roles, others celebrate female divinity and power. Feminist and reform movements within Hinduism seek to challenge patriarchal interpretations and promote gender equality.

- **Buddhism:** Buddhism's teachings on compassion and non-attachment provide a basis for challenging gender discrimination. However, historical practices have often excluded women from monastic life and leadership. Contemporary movements within Buddhism advocate for the inclusion and ordination of women and emphasize gender equality.

- **Indigenous Religions:** Indigenous spiritual traditions often hold unique perspectives on gender, recognizing the interconnectedness of all life and the importance of balance and harmony. These traditions can offer valuable insights into holistic and egalitarian approaches to gender relations.

## Spirituality and Gender Liberation

Beyond organized religion, spirituality offers diverse pathways for exploring and transforming gender dynamics. Personal spiritual practices, new religious movements, and holistic approaches to well-being often emphasize principles of equality, respect, and empowerment.

- **Personal Spiritual Practices:** Many individuals draw on personal spiritual practices, such as meditation, yoga, and mindfulness, to explore their identities and challenge restrictive gender norms. These practices can promote self-awareness, healing, and empowerment.

- **New Religious Movements:** New religious movements and spiritual communities often emphasize inclusivity, social justice, and personal transformation. These movements provide alternative frameworks for understanding and practicing gender equality.

- **Holistic Approaches to Well-being:** Holistic approaches to well-being, which integrate physical, emotional, and spiritual health, often advocate for gender equality as part of a broader commitment to social justice and human flourishing. These approaches emphasize the interconnectedness of personal and societal transformation.

## Philosophical and Ethical Perspectives on Religion and Gender

Philosophical and ethical frameworks offer valuable insights into the principles and values that underpin gender dynamics within religious and spiritual contexts. Key perspectives include:

- **Feminist Theology and Ethics:** Feminist theology and ethics challenge patriarchal interpretations of religious texts and traditions, advocating for the equal treatment and participation of women. This perspective emphasizes the importance of justice, equality, and mutual respect within religious and spiritual communities.

- **Liberation Theology:** Liberation theology focuses on the liberation of oppressed groups, including women, through a commitment to social justice and human dignity. This perspective draws on religious teachings to advocate for structural and systemic change.

- **Interfaith Dialogue:** Interfaith dialogue promotes understanding and collaboration among different religious and spiritual traditions. By fostering mutual respect and shared values, interfaith dialogue can support efforts to promote gender equality and challenge discriminatory practices.

- **Spiritual Humanism:** Spiritual humanism emphasizes the inherent worth and dignity of all individuals, advocating for equality and social justice. This perspective integrates spiritual and humanistic principles to promote holistic well-being and gender liberation.

## Case Studies and Examples

Examining case studies and examples of gender equality initiatives within religious and spiritual contexts provides practical insights into the challenges and successes of these efforts. Examples include:

- **Women Religious Leaders:** Highlighting the stories of women who have assumed leadership roles within their religious communities, such as female priests, imams, rabbis, and spiritual teachers, demonstrates the potential for change and the impact of gender-inclusive leadership.

- **Gender-Inclusive Worship Practices:** Exploring initiatives that promote gender-inclusive worship practices, such as inclusive language, rituals that honor women's experiences, and the participation of women in religious ceremonies, illustrates how traditions can be adapted to support gender equality.

- **Interfaith Initiatives for Gender Justice:** Showcasing interfaith initiatives that address gender-based violence, support women's empowerment, and promote gender equality highlights the potential for collaborative efforts across religious and spiritual traditions.

**- Community-Based Spiritual Movements:** Examining community-based spiritual movements that emphasize gender equality, social justice, and holistic well-being provides examples of how grassroots efforts can drive meaningful change.

## Conclusion: Embracing Gender Equality in Religion and Spirituality

Religion and spirituality have profound impacts on gender dynamics, shaping how individuals and communities understand and practice gender roles. While traditional interpretations have often reinforced patriarchal norms, contemporary movements and reinterpretations offer pathways for promoting gender equality and liberation.

By engaging with religious teachings, fostering inclusive practices, and embracing intersectional perspectives, individuals and communities can challenge discriminatory norms and create more equitable and supportive environments. Philosophical and ethical frameworks provide valuable guidance for navigating these complexities and advocating for justice, dignity, and mutual respect.

Ultimately, the role of religion and spirituality in promoting gender equality reflects a broader commitment to human flourishing and social justice. By integrating spiritual principles with practical efforts for change, we can work towards a future where all individuals, regardless of gender, can thrive and contribute to a more just and compassionate world.

# Chapter Nine

# Addressing Gender Bias and Moving Forward

## Introduction to Gender Bias

Gender bias, the preferential treatment or unfair disadvantage of individuals based on their gender, remains a significant barrier to achieving true equality. Despite the progress made in recent decades, gender bias persists in various forms, affecting education, the workplace, media representation, and interpersonal relationships. This chapter explores comprehensive strategies to address gender bias and outlines the steps needed to move forward towards a more equitable society. The focus will be on achieving gender balance, implementing educational and social reforms, and drawing on philosophical and inspirational guidance to inspire change.

## Strategies for Achieving Gender Balance

Addressing gender bias requires multi-faceted strategies that target the root causes and manifestations of inequality. Here are several key approaches to achieving gender balance:

## 1. Policy and Legislative Reforms

- **Equal Pay Legislation:** Governments should enforce and enhance laws that mandate equal pay for equal work, ensuring that wage gaps between men and women are closed. Regular audits and transparency in pay structures can help in monitoring compliance.

- **Anti-Discrimination Laws:** Strengthening anti-discrimination laws to protect individuals from gender-based discrimination in all areas, including employment, education, and public services, is crucial. These laws should be supported by robust enforcement mechanisms and accessible reporting channels.

- **Parental Leave Policies:** Implementing equitable parental leave policies that encourage both parents to participate in child-rearing can help balance domestic responsibilities. Paid parental leave for both mothers and fathers promotes gender equality at home and in the workplace.

## 2. Organizational Practices

- **Diversity and Inclusion Training:** Organizations should invest in regular training programs focused on diversity, equity, and inclusion. These programs should educate employees about unconscious bias, promote inclusive behaviors, and foster a culture of respect and equality.

- **Mentorship and Sponsorship Programs:** Establishing mentorship and sponsorship programs for women and underrepresented groups can help in career advancement and breaking the glass ceiling. These programs should be designed to provide guidance, support, and networking opportunities.

- **Flexible Work Arrangements:** Providing flexible work options, such as remote work, flexible hours, and part-time positions, can help accommodate the diverse needs of employees. These arrangements are particularly beneficial for those balancing work and family responsibilities.

## 3. Representation and Leadership

- **Gender Parity in Leadership:** Promoting gender parity in leadership positions across sectors is essential for creating role models and driving organizational change. Quotas and targets can be effective tools in achieving balanced representation on boards and executive teams.

- **Visible Role Models:** Highlighting the achievements of successful women and gender-diverse individuals in various fields can inspire the next generation and challenge stereotypes. Media, educational institutions, and organizations should actively promote diverse role models.

## 4. Community and Grassroots Initiatives

- **Local Advocacy Groups:** Supporting and collaborating with local advocacy groups that work on gender equality issues can amplify efforts and create a more significant impact. These groups often have the contextual knowledge and grassroots connections necessary for effective change.

- **Public Awareness Campaigns:** Launching public awareness campaigns to educate communities about gender bias and promote gender equality can shift societal attitudes. These campaigns should utilize various media platforms to reach a broad audience.

Educational and social reforms are fundamental to dismantling gender bias and promoting equality from an early age. Here are several key areas of focus:

## 1. Curriculum and Pedagogy

- **Inclusive Curriculum:** Schools and educational institutions should adopt an inclusive curriculum that reflects diverse perspectives and experiences. This includes integrating gender studies into the curriculum and teaching about the contributions of women and gender-diverse individuals in various fields.

- **Gender-Sensitive Pedagogy:** Teachers should be trained in gender-sensitive pedagogy that promotes equality and challenges stereotypes. This includes using inclusive language, addressing gender bias in classroom interactions, and encouraging all students to participate in all activities.

- **STEM Education:** Encouraging girls and women to pursue education and careers in STEM (Science, Technology, Engineering, and

Mathematics) fields is critical. Initiatives such as scholarships, mentorship programs, and STEM clubs can help bridge the gender gap in these areas.

## 2. Early Childhood Education

- **Challenging Stereotypes Early:** Early childhood education should focus on challenging gender stereotypes and promoting equality from a young age. This includes providing diverse toys, books, and activities that encourage all children to explore a wide range of interests and skills.

- **Parental Involvement:** Educating parents about gender bias and encouraging them to raise their children with egalitarian values is crucial. Parenting programs and resources can help parents support their children's development in an unbiased and inclusive manner.

## 3. Higher Education and Research

- **Gender Studies Programs:** Expanding gender studies programs at universities can provide students with a deeper understanding of gender issues and prepare them to contribute to gender equality efforts in their professional and personal lives.

- **Research on Gender Equality:** Funding and supporting research on gender equality and the impacts of gender bias can inform policy and practice. This research should be interdisciplinary and inclusive, addressing the experiences of all genders.

## 4. Media and Representation

- **Media Literacy Education:** Teaching media literacy in schools can help students critically analyze media representations of gender and recognize bias and stereotypes. Media literacy programs should empower students to create and share diverse and inclusive content.

- **Positive Media Representation:** Media organizations should strive to portray diverse and positive representations of all genders. This includes producing content that challenges stereotypes, highlights gender equality, and features strong, multidimensional characters.

## 5. Social Norms and Cultural Change

- **Community Engagement:** Engaging communities in discussions about gender norms and biases can foster cultural change. Community leaders, religious organizations, and cultural institutions can play a pivotal role in promoting gender equality.

**- Challenging Toxic Masculinity:** Addressing toxic masculinity and promoting healthy, positive models of masculinity is essential for gender equality. Programs that encourage men to express emotions, participate in caregiving, and reject violence and aggression can help reshape social norms.

## Philosophical and Inspirational Guidance for Change

Philosophical and inspirational guidance can provide the ethical foundation and motivation needed to pursue gender equality. Drawing on various philosophical traditions and inspirational figures can offer valuable insights and encouragement.

### 1. Feminist Philosophy

**- Ethics of Care:** The ethics of care, as articulated by feminist philosophers such as Carol Gilligan and Nel Noddings, emphasizes the importance of relationships, empathy, and compassion in ethical decision-making. This perspective encourages individuals and institutions to prioritize care and mutual support in their actions.

- **Intersectional Feminism:** Intersectional feminism, championed by scholars like Kimberlé Crenshaw, highlights the interconnectedness of various forms of oppression and the need to address multiple axes of identity, including race, class, and sexuality, in the pursuit of gender equality.

## 2. Human Rights and Social Justice

- **Universal Human Rights:** The principles of universal human rights, as outlined in documents such as the Universal Declaration of Human Rights, provide a framework for advocating gender equality. These principles affirm the inherent dignity and equality of all individuals, regardless of gender.

- **Social Justice Movements:** Social justice movements, including civil rights, LGBTQ+ rights, and disability rights, offer valuable lessons and strategies for advocating gender equality. These movements emphasize the importance of collective action, allyship, and systemic change.

## 3. Inspirational Figures

- **Historical and Contemporary Leaders:** Highlighting the contributions of historical and contemporary leaders in the fight for gender equality can provide inspiration and motivation. Figures such as Sojourner Truth, Emmeline Pankhurst, Malala Yousafzai, and Ruth Bader Ginsburg have made significant impacts and serve as role models.

- **Everyday Heroes:** Recognizing and celebrating the efforts of everyday heroes who work towards gender equality in their communities, workplaces, and families can inspire others to take action. These individuals demonstrate that everyone has the power to contribute to positive change.

## 4. Philosophical Traditions

- **Virtue Ethics:** Virtue ethics, as developed by philosophers like Aristotle, emphasizes the cultivation of moral virtues such as courage, justice, and compassion. Applying virtue ethics to gender equality encourages individuals to strive for personal excellence and ethical behavior in their interactions.

- **Existentialist Perspectives:** Existentialist philosophers such as Jean-Paul Sartre and

Simone de Beauvoir explore themes of freedom, responsibility, and authenticity. These perspectives emphasize the importance of challenging societal norms and creating authentic, equitable relationships.

## Conclusion: Moving Forward Towards Gender Equality

Addressing gender bias and achieving gender equality is a complex and ongoing process that requires concerted efforts across multiple levels of society. By implementing comprehensive strategies for achieving gender balance, pursuing educational and social reforms, and drawing on philosophical and inspirational guidance, we can create a more equitable and inclusive world.

Moving forward, it is essential to remain vigilant in identifying and challenging gender bias in all its forms. This includes continuing to advocate for policy and legislative reforms, fostering inclusive organizational practices, promoting gender equality in education, and reshaping cultural and media representations.

Ultimately, the pursuit of gender equality is not only a matter of justice but also a means to enrich and strengthen our societies. By embracing diversity, fostering mutual respect, and working together towards common goals, we can create a future where all individuals, regardless of gender, can thrive and contribute to a more just and compassionate world.

# Conclusion

## Recap of Key Points

Throughout this book, we have explored the multifaceted issue of gender bias and the persistent inequalities that stem from it. Here, we revisit the key points discussed in each chapter to reaffirm our understanding and commitment to fostering a gender-equal society:

1. **Historical Context of Gender Roles:** We examined the historical foundations of gender roles, tracing how ancient cultures and societies established and perpetuated gender norms that still influence modern perceptions.

2. **Modern Society and Gender Perceptions:** This chapter delved into the ways contemporary society continues to grapple with gender stereotypes and biases, highlighting both progress and ongoing challenges in achieving true equality.

**3. Gender Bias in Education and Workforce:** We analyzed how gender bias manifests in educational settings and workplaces, affecting opportunities, representation, and treatment of individuals based on gender.

**4. Media, Culture, and Gender Stereotypes:** The impact of media and cultural narratives on reinforcing gender stereotypes was explored, emphasizing the need for more balanced and inclusive representations.

**5. Gender and Emotional Well-being:** This chapter focused on how gender expectations affect emotional health and well-being, discussing the unique challenges faced by different genders and the importance of emotional literacy and support.

**6. Legal and Policy Frameworks:** We reviewed existing legal and policy frameworks aimed at addressing gender bias and promoting equality, and discussed the gaps and opportunities for further reform.

**7. Gender Dynamics in Relationships:** The dynamics of gender in personal and romantic relationships were examined, highlighting how power imbalances and societal expectations influence relationships.

8. **The Role of Religion and Spirituality:** This chapter considered the complex role of religion and spirituality in shaping gender roles and how religious and spiritual beliefs can both reinforce and challenge gender norms.

9. **Addressing Gender Bias and Moving Forward:** Strategies for achieving gender balance were outlined, including educational and social reforms, and philosophical and inspirational guidance for fostering change.

10. **Promoting Gender Equality Through Media and Cultural Change:** We discussed the importance of media and culture in shaping societal attitudes towards gender and the steps needed to promote equality through these channels.

## Vision for a Balanced Society

Our vision for a balanced society is one where gender equality is not just an ideal but a lived reality. In this society:

- **Equality in Opportunities:** All individuals have equal access to education, employment, and leadership positions, regardless of gender. Opportunities are based on merit and capability, not biased expectations or stereotypes.

- **Inclusive Education:** Educational systems are reformed to include gender-sensitive curricula and pedagogies that challenge stereotypes and promote critical thinking about gender.

- **Equitable Workplaces:** Work environments are designed to be inclusive and supportive, with policies that ensure equal pay, flexible work arrangements, and opportunities for career advancement for all genders.

- **Balanced Media Representation:** Media and cultural narratives reflect the diversity of human experiences, portraying all genders in multidimensional and empowering roles, thereby influencing public perception positively.

- **Healthy Relationships:** Personal and romantic relationships are based on mutual respect, equality, and shared responsibilities. Societal norms support balanced partnerships where emotional well-being is prioritized.

- **Supportive Legal Frameworks:** Robust legal and policy frameworks protect against gender discrimination and promote equality. These frameworks are actively enforced and continuously updated to address emerging issues.

- **Empowered Individuals:** Everyone is encouraged and supported to pursue their passions and goals without the constraints of restrictive gender norms. Emotional well-being and mental health are prioritized and supported.

## Final Thoughts and Inspirational Messages

Achieving gender equality is a collective journey that requires dedication, empathy, and action from all sectors of society. While the path is challenging, it is also filled with opportunities for growth and transformation. Here are some final thoughts and inspirational messages to guide us on this journey:

- **Believe in Change:** Change is possible, and each step towards gender equality makes a difference. Believe in the power of individual and collective actions to create a more just and balanced world.

- **Embrace Diversity:** Diversity is a strength. Embrace and celebrate the unique perspectives and contributions of all genders, recognizing that inclusion enriches our communities and drives innovation and progress.

- **Lead by Example:** Be a role model for gender equality in your personal and professional life. Challenge stereotypes, speak out against discrimination, and support policies and practices that promote fairness and inclusion.

- **Educate and Advocate**: Continue to educate yourself and others about gender issues. Advocacy and awareness are crucial for driving societal change and inspiring future generations to uphold the values of equality and justice.

- **Foster Empathy:** Cultivate empathy and understanding. Listen to the experiences of others, especially those different from your own, and use that understanding to build bridges and foster solidarity.

- **Stay Resilient:** The journey towards gender equality is long and filled with obstacles, but resilience and perseverance are key. Stay committed to the cause, even when progress seems slow, and celebrate every victory along the way.

- **Hope for the Future:** Maintain hope for a future where gender equality is the norm, not the exception. This vision can inspire and sustain us as we work towards creating a world where everyone can thrive, free from the constraints of gender bias.

In closing, the pursuit of gender equality is a noble and necessary endeavor that benefits all of humanity. By addressing gender bias and promoting inclusive practices, we move closer to a society where everyone can realize their full potential. Let us continue to strive for a world where equality, respect, and justice prevail, and where the diversity of all genders is recognized and celebrated. Together, we can create a brighter, more equitable future for all.

* 9 7 9 8 3 3 3 6 0 9 5 5 7 *